Explore this great collection of Kids' Snuggies. Each of these seven crochet p
from Lisa Gentry produces a fun design that is just right for kids. Whether reading a book, watching a movie, or just hanging out, kids will have a warm, fantastic time in any of these Snuggies. Choose the design and the yarn weight and color combinations for the look your little one most desires.

LEISURE ARTS, INC.
Maumelle, Arkansas

Princess Dress

EASY **Finished Size:** 15" across Yoke x 43" long (38 cm x 109 cm)

SHOPPING LIST

Yarn (Bulky Weight) BULKY 5

[5 ounces, 131 yards
(141 grams, 120 meters) per skein]:

- ☐ Purple - 4 skeins
- ☐ White - 3 skeins

Crochet Hooks

- ☐ Size K (6.5 mm) **and**
- ☐ Size L (8 mm)
  or sizes needed for gauge

Additional Supplies

- ☐ Safety pin
- ☐ Yarn needle

GAUGE INFORMATION

With larger size hook, in pattern,
9 sts and 4 rows = 4" (10 cm)

Gauge Swatch: 4" (10 cm)
With larger size hook, ch 11.
Row 1: Dc in fourth ch from hook and in each ch across **(3 skipped chs count as first dc)**: 9 dc.
Rows 2-6: Ch 3 **(counts as first dc)**, turn; dc in next dc and in each dc across.
Finish off.

STITCH GUIDE

TREBLE CROCHET ***(abbreviated tr)***
YO twice, insert hook in st or sp indicated, YO and pull up a loop (4 loops on hook), (YO and draw through 2 loops on hook) 3 times.

SINGLE CROCHET 2 TOGETHER ***(abbreviated sc2tog)***
Pull up a loop in each of next 2 dc, YO and draw through all 3 loops on hook **(counts as one sc)**.

SINGLE CROCHET 3 TOGETHER ***(abbreviated sc3tog)***
Pull up a loop in each of next 3 dc, YO and draw through all 4 loops on hook (**counts as one sc**).

DOUBLE CROCHET 2 TOGETHER ***(abbreviated dc2tog)***
(uses next 2 dc)
★ YO, insert hook in **next** dc, YO and pull up a loop, YO and draw through 2 loops on hook; repeat from ★ once **more**, YO and draw through all 3 loops on hook **(counts as one dc)**.

DOUBLE CROCHET 3 TOGETHER ***(abbreviated dc3tog)***
(uses next 3 sts)
★ YO, insert hook in **next** st, YO and pull up a loop, YO and draw through 2 loops on hook; repeat from ★ 2 times **more**, YO and draw through all 4 loops on hook **(counts as one dc)**.

PICOT
Ch 3, slip st in third ch from hook.

BODY

With larger size hook and Purple, ch 91.

Row 1 (Right side)**:** Sc in second ch from hook, (skip next 2 chs, 3 sc in next ch) 3 times, (skip next 2 chs, 3 hdc in next ch) 5 times, (skip next 2 chs, 3 dc in next ch) 10 times, (skip next 2 chs, 3 tr in next ch) 11 times, skip next ch, tr in last ch: 89 sts.

Note: Loop a short piece of yarn around any stitch to mark Row 1 as **right** side.

Row 2: Ch 6, turn; skip next tr, (dc, ch 1, dc) in next tr, **[**skip next 2 sts, (dc, ch 1, dc) in next st**]** 25 times, **[**skip next 2 sts, (hdc, ch 1, hdc) in next st**]** 3 times, skip next sc, sc in last sc: 59 sts, 29 ch-1 sps, and one ch-6 sp.

Row 3: Ch 1, turn; sc in first sc, 3 sc in each of next 3 ch-1 sps, 3 hdc in each of next 5 ch-1 sps, 3 dc in each of next 10 ch-1 sps, 3 tr in each of next 11 ch-1 sps, tr in last ch-6 sp: 89 sts.

Rows 4-8: Repeat Rows 2 and 3 twice, then repeat Row 2 once **more**.

Finish off.

Row 9: With **right** side facing, join White with sc in first sc ***(see Joining With Sc, page 42)***; 3 sc in each of next 8 ch-1 sps, 3 hdc in each of next 6 ch-1 sps, 3 dc in each of next 4 ch-1 sps, 3 tr in each of next 11 ch-1 sps, tr in last ch-6 sp: 89 sts.

Row 10: Ch 6, turn; skip next tr, (dc, ch 1, dc) in next tr, **[**skip next 2 sts, (dc, ch 1, dc) in next st**]** 14 times, **[**skip next 2 sts, (hdc, ch 1, hdc) in next st**]** 4 times, skip next 2 sts, sc in next st, place marker around sc just made, leave remaining sts unworked: 39 sts, 19 ch-1 sps, and one ch-6 sp.

Row 11: Ch 1, turn; skip first sc, 3 sc in each of next 2 ch-1 sps, 3 hdc in each of next 2 ch-1 sps, 3 dc in each of next 4 ch-1 sps, 3 tr in each of next 11 ch-1 sps, tr in last ch-6 sp: 58 sts.

Row 12: Ch 6, turn; skip next tr, (dc, ch 1, dc) in next tr, **[**skip next 2 sts, (dc, ch 1, dc) in next st**]** 14 times, **[**skip next 2 sts, (hdc, ch 1, hdc) in next st**]** 4 times, working in sts on previous row, (hdc, ch 1, hdc) in same st as marked st, **[**skip next 2 sts, (hdc, ch 1, hdc) in next st**]** 9 times, skip next sc, sc in last sc: 59 sts, 29 ch-1 sps, and one ch-6 sp.

Row 13: Ch 1, turn; sc in first sc, 3 sc in each of next 8 ch-1 sps, 3 hdc in each of next 6 ch-1 sps, 3 dc in each of next 4 ch-1 sps, 3 tr in each of next 11 ch-1 sps, tr in last ch-6 sp: 89 sts.

Row 14: Ch 6, turn; skip next tr, (dc, ch 1, dc) in next tr, **[**skip next 2 sts, (dc, ch 1, dc) in next st**]** 14 times, **[**skip next 2 sts, (hdc, ch 1, hdc) in next st**]** 14 times, skip next sc, sc in last sc; finish off: 59 sts, 29 ch-1 sps, and one ch-6 sp.

Row 15: With **right** side facing, join Purple with sc in first sc; 3 sc in each of next 3 ch-1 sps, 3 hdc in each of next 5 ch-1 sps, 3 dc in each of next 10 ch-1 sps, 3 tr in each of next 11 ch-1 sps, tr in last ch-6 sp: 89 sts.

Rows 16-18: Repeat Rows 2 and 3 once, then repeat Row 2 once **more**.

Finish off.

Rows 19-25: Repeat Rows 9-15.

Rows 26-30: Repeat Rows 2 and 3 twice, then repeat Row 2 once **more**.

Finish off.

Rows 31-47: Repeat Rows 9-25.

Rows 48-53: Repeat Rows 2 and 3, 3 times.

Finish off.

YOKE

Row 1: With **right** side of top edge facing and using larger size hook, with White, ch 39 loosely (first sleeve), work 32 sc evenly spaced across ends of rows.

Row 2: Ch 41 loosely (second sleeve), turn; dc in fourth ch from hook and in next 35 chs, dc3tog (worked over next 2 chs and next sc), dc in next 30 sc, dc3tog (worked over next sc and next 2 chs), dc in next 37 chs: 106 dc.

Row 3: Ch 3 **(counts as first dc, now and throughout)**, turn; dc2tog, dc in next 33 dc, dc3tog, dc in next 28 dc, dc3tog, dc in next 34 dc, dc2tog: 100 dc.

Row 4: Ch 3, turn; dc2tog, dc in next 31 dc, dc3tog, dc in next 26 dc, dc3tog, dc in next 32 dc, dc2tog: 94 dc.

Row 5: Ch 3, turn; dc2tog, dc in next 29 dc, dc3tog, dc in next 24 dc, dc3tog, dc in next 30 dc, dc2tog: 88 dc.

Row 6: Ch 3, turn; dc2tog, dc in next 27 dc, dc3tog, dc in next 22 dc, dc3tog, dc in next 28 dc, dc2tog: 82 dc.

Row 7: Ch 1, turn; beginning in first dc, sc2tog, sc in next 26 dc, sc3tog, sc in next 20 dc, sc3tog, sc in next 26 dc, sc2tog: 76 sc.

Finish off.

Fold each sleeve to **wrong** side and sew in place.

BOTTOM EDGING

Row 1: With **right** side facing, using smaller size hook, and working in ends of rows, join White with sc around tr on Row 1; 2 sc around same tr, ★ ch 1, working in **front** of ch-6 sp on next row, 3 tr around next dc, ch 1, 3 sc around tr on next row; repeat from ★ across; place loop from hook onto safety pin to keep piece from unraveling while you work next row.

Row 2: With **right** side facing and using smaller size hook, join Purple with sc in first sc; skip next 3 sts, (3 dc, ch 1, 3 dc) in next tr (center tr), ★ skip next 2 sts, sc in next sc, skip next 2 sts, (3 dc, ch 1, 3 dc) in next tr; repeat from ★ across to last 4 sts, skip next 3 sts, sc in last sc; finish off.

Row 3: Slip loop from safety pin onto smaller size hook, ch 4, turn; dc in first sc, ★ ch 3, sc in next ch-1 sp, ch 3, skip next 3 dc, (dc, ch 1, dc) in next sc; repeat from ★ across; finish off.

OUTER TRIM

With **wrong** side of Yoke facing and using smaller size hook, join Purple with sc in free loop of first ch on second sleeve ***(Fig. 3, page 44)***; sc in free loop of each ch across and in each st across to Bottom Edging; sc in end of Row 1, (3 dc, work Picot, 3 dc) in same sp, ★ ch 1, skip next dc, slip st in next sc, ch 1, skip next ch-3 sp, (3 dc, work Picot, 3 dc) in next ch-1 sp; repeat from ★ across; sc in end of Row 1 of Bottom Edging and in free loop of each ch across Body and first sleeve; finish off.

NECK TRIM

With **wrong** side of Yoke facing and using smaller size hook, join Purple with sc in first sc on first sleeve; sc in each sc across; finish off.

BOW

With smaller size hook and Purple, make an adjustable loop to form a ring ***(Figs. 1a-d, page 43)***; (ch 3, 3 tr, ch 3, slip st) twice in ring; finish off leaving a long end to form center.

Wrap end around center 3 times and secure end; do **not** cut yarn.

Using photo as a guide for placement, sew Bow to front of Yoke.

Ice Cream Cone

EASY +

Finished Size: 62" circumference at top edge of Waffle Cone x 50" long (157.5 cm x 127 cm)

SHOPPING LIST

Yarn (Bulky Weight)

BULKY 5

[3 ounces, 156 yards (85 grams, 143 meters) per skein]:

- ☐ Tan - 5 skeins
- ☐ Variegated - 5 skeins

Crochet Hook

- ☐ Size L (8 mm) **or** size needed for gauge

Additional Supplies

- ☐ Yarn needle

GAUGE INFORMATION

9 dc and 6 rows = 4" (10 cm)

Gauge Swatch: 4" (10 cm) square

Ch 11.

Row 1: Dc in fourth ch from hook and in each ch across **(3 skipped chs count as first dc)**: 9 dc.

Rows 2-6: Ch 3 **(counts as first dc)**, turn; dc in next dc and in each dc across.

Finish off.

STITCH GUIDE

FRONT POST DOUBLE CROCHET *(abbreviated FPdc)*

YO, insert hook from **front** to **back** around post of st indicated ***(Fig. 4, page 44)***, YO and pull up a loop (3 loops on hook), (YO and draw through 2 loops on hook) twice.

BACK POST DOUBLE CROCHET *(abbreviated BPdc)*

YO, insert hook from **back** to **front** around post of st indicated ***(Fig. 4, page 44)***, YO and pull up a loop (3 loops on hook), (YO and draw through 2 loops on hook) twice.

BODY (Make 2)
WAFFLE CONE

With Tan, ch 3; join with slip st to form a ring.

Row 1 (Right side)**:** Ch 2 **(counts as first dc, now and throughout Waffle Cone)**, 7 dc in ring; do **not** join: 8 dc.

Note: Loop a short piece of yarn around any stitch to mark Row 1 as **right** side.

Row 2: Ch 2, turn; work BPdc around next dc, (dc in next dc, work BPdc around same dc just worked into) across to last dc, dc in last dc: 13 sts.

Row 3: Ch 2, turn; (work FPdc around next BPdc, dc in next dc) across.

Row 4: Ch 2, turn; (work BPdc around next FPdc, dc in next dc) across.

Row 5: Ch 2, turn; work FPdc around next BPdc, (2 dc in next dc, work FPdc around next BPdc) across to last dc, dc in last dc: 18 sts.

Row 6: Ch 2, turn; work BPdc around next FPdc, (dc in next 2 dc, work BPdc around next FPdc) across to last dc, dc in last dc.

Row 7: Ch 2, turn; work FPdc around next BPdc, ★ work BPdc around each of next 2 dc, work FPdc around next BPdc; repeat from ★ across to last dc, dc in last dc.

Row 8: Ch 2, turn; work BPdc around next FPdc, ★ 2 dc in next BPdc, dc in next BPdc, work BPdc around next FPdc; repeat from ★ across to last dc, dc in last dc: 23 sts.

Row 9: Ch 2, turn; work FPdc around next BPdc, (dc in next 3 dc, work FPdc around next BPdc) across to last dc, dc in last dc.

Row 10: Ch 2, turn; work BPdc around next FPdc, (dc in next 3 dc, work BPdc around next FPdc) across to last dc, dc in last dc.

Row 11: Ch 2, turn; work FPdc around next BPdc, (2 dc in next dc, dc in next 2 dc, work FPdc around next BPdc) across to last dc, dc in last dc: 28 sts.

Row 12: Ch 2, turn; work BPdc around next FPdc, (dc in next 4 dc, work BPdc around next FPdc) across to last dc, dc in last dc.

Row 13: Ch 2, turn; work FPdc around next BPdc, (dc in next 4 dc, work FPdc around next BPdc) across to last dc, dc in last dc.

Row 14: Ch 2, turn; work BPdc around next FPdc, (2 dc in next dc, dc in next 3 dc, work BPdc around next FPdc) across to last dc, dc in last dc: 33 sts.

Row 15: Ch 2, turn; work FPdc around next BPdc, (work BPdc around each of next 5 dc, work FPdc around next BPdc) across to last dc, dc in last dc.

Row 16: Ch 2, turn; work BPdc around next FPdc, (dc in next 5 BPdc, work BPdc around next FPdc) across to last dc, dc in last dc.

Row 17: Ch 2, turn; work FPdc around next BPdc, ★ 2 dc in next dc, dc in next 4 dc, work FPdc around next BPdc; repeat from ★ across to last dc, dc in last dc: 38 sts.

Row 18: Ch 2, turn; work BPdc around next FPdc, (dc in next 6 dc, work BPdc around next FPdc) across to last dc, dc in last dc.

Row 19: Ch 2, turn; work FPdc around next BPdc, (dc in next 6 dc, work FPdc around next BPdc) across to last dc, dc in last dc.

Row 20: Ch 2, turn; work BPdc around next FPdc, ★ 2 dc in next dc, dc in next 5 dc, work BPdc around next FPdc; repeat from ★ across to last dc, dc in last dc: 43 sts.

Row 21: Ch 2, turn; work FPdc around next BPdc, (dc in next 7 dc, work FPdc around next BPdc) across to last dc, dc in last dc.

Row 22: Ch 2, turn; work BPdc around next FPdc, (dc in next 7 dc, work BPdc around next FPdc) across to last dc, dc in last dc.

Row 23: Ch 2, turn; work FPdc around next BPdc, ★ work BPdc around each of next 7 dc, dc in next BPdc, work FPdc around same BPdc just worked into; repeat from ★ across to last dc, dc in last dc: 48 sts.

Row 24: Ch 2, turn; work BPdc around next FPdc, (dc in next 8 sts, work BPdc around next FPdc) across to last dc, dc in last dc.

Row 25: Ch 2, turn; work FPdc around next BPdc, (dc in next 8 dc, work FPdc around next BPdc) across to last dc, dc in last dc.

Row 26: Ch 2, turn; work BPdc around next FPdc, ★ 2 dc in next dc, dc in next 7 dc, work BPdc around next FPdc; repeat from ★ across to last dc, dc in last dc: 53 sts.

Row 27: Ch 2, turn; work FPdc around next BPdc, (dc in next 9 dc, work FPdc around next BPdc) across to last dc, dc in last dc.

Row 28: Ch 2, turn; work BPdc around next FPdc, (dc in next 9 dc, work BPdc around next FPdc) across to last dc, dc in last dc.

Row 29: Ch 2, turn; work FPdc around next BPdc, ★ 2 dc in next dc, dc in next 8 dc, work FPdc around next BPdc; repeat from ★ across to last dc, dc in last dc: 58 sts.

Row 30: Ch 2, turn; work BPdc around next FPdc, (dc in next 10 dc, work BPdc around next FPdc) across to last dc, dc in last dc.

Row 31: Ch 2, turn; work FPdc around next BPdc, ★ work BPdc around each of next 10 dc, work FPdc around next BPdc; repeat from ★ across to last dc, dc in last dc.

Row 32: Ch 2, turn; work BPdc around next FPdc, ★ 2 dc in next BPdc, dc in next 9 BPdc, work BPdc around next FPdc; repeat from ★ across to last dc, dc in last dc: 63 sts.

Row 33: Ch 2, turn; work FPdc around next BPdc, (dc in next 11 dc, work FPdc around next BPdc) across to last dc, dc in last dc.

Row 34: Ch 2, turn; work BPdc around next FPdc, (dc in next 11 dc, work BPdc around next FPdc) across to last dc, dc in last dc.

Row 35: Ch 2, turn; work FPdc around next BPdc, ★ 2 dc in next dc, dc in next 10 dc, work FPdc around next BPdc; repeat from ★ across to last dc, dc in last dc: 68 sts.

Row 36: Ch 2, turn; work BPdc around next FPdc, (dc in next 12 dc, work BPdc around next FPdc) across to last dc, dc in last dc.

Row 37: Ch 2, turn; work FPdc around next BPdc, (dc in next 12 dc, work FPdc around next BPdc) across to last dc, dc in last dc.

Row 38: Ch 2, turn; work BPdc around next FPdc, ★ 2 dc in next dc, dc in next 11 dc, work BPdc around next FPdc; repeat from ★ across to last dc, dc in last dc: 73 sts.

Row 39: Ch 2, turn; work FPdc around next BPdc, (work BPdc around each of next 13 dc, work FPdc around next BPdc) across to last dc, dc in last dc.

Row 40: Ch 2, turn; work BPdc around next FPdc, (dc in next 6 dc, work BPdc around next st) across to last dc, dc in last dc.

Row 41: Ch 2, turn; work FPdc around next BPdc, (dc in next 6 dc, work FPdc around next BPdc) across to last dc, dc in last dc.

Row 42: Ch 2, turn; work BPdc around next FPdc, (dc in next 6 dc, work BPdc around next FPdc) across to last dc, dc in last dc.

Row 43: Ch 2, turn; work FPdc around next BPdc, ★ work BPdc around each of next 6 dc, work FPdc around next BPdc; repeat from ★ across to last dc, dc in last dc.

Row 44: Ch 2, turn; work BPdc around next FPdc, (dc in next 6 BPdc, work BPdc around next FPdc) across to last dc, dc in last dc.

Rows 45-50: Repeat Rows 41-44 once, then repeat Rows 41 and 42 once **more**.

Finish off.

SCOOP

With Variegated, ch 4.

Row 1: 7 Dc in fourth ch from hook **(3 skipped chs counts as first dc)**; do **not** join: 8 dc.

Row 2 (Right side)**:** Ch 3 **(counts as first dc, now and throughout)**, turn; 2 dc in each of next 6 dc, dc in last dc: 14 dc.

Note: Mark Row 2 as **right** side.

Row 3: Ch 3, turn; (dc in next dc, 2 dc in next dc) across: 21 dc.

Row 4: Ch 3, turn; dc in next dc, 2 dc in next dc, (dc in next 2 dc, 2 dc in next dc) across: 28 dc.

Row 5: Ch 3, turn; (2 dc in next dc, dc in next 2 dc) across: 37 dc.

Row 6: Ch 3, turn; dc in next 2 dc, 2 dc in next dc, (dc in next 4 dc, 2 dc in next dc) across to last 3 dc, dc in last 3 dc: 44 dc.

Row 7: Ch 3, turn; dc in next 3 dc, 2 dc in next dc, (dc in next 5 dc, 2 dc in next dc) across to last 3 dc, dc in last 3 dc: 51 dc.

Row 8: Ch 3, turn; dc in next 3 dc, 2 dc in next dc, (dc in next 6 dc, 2 dc in next dc) across to last 4 dc, dc in last 4 dc: 58 dc.

Row 9: Ch 3, turn; dc in next 4 dc, 2 dc in next dc, (dc in next 7 dc, 2 dc in next dc) across to last 4 dc, dc in last 4 dc: 65 dc.

Row 10: Ch 3, turn; dc in next 4 dc, 2 dc in next dc, (dc in next 8 dc, 2 dc in next dc) across to last 5 dc, dc in last 5 dc: 72 dc.

Row 11: Ch 3, turn; dc in next 5 dc, 2 dc in next dc, (dc in next 9 dc, 2 dc in next dc) across to last 5 dc, dc in last 5 dc: 79 dc.

Row 12: Ch 3, turn; dc in next 5 dc, 2 dc in next dc, (dc in next 10 dc, 2 dc in next dc) across to last 6 dc, dc in last 6 dc: 86 dc.

Row 13: Ch 3, turn; dc in next 6 dc, 2 dc in next dc, (dc in next 11 dc, 2 dc in next dc) across to last 6 dc, dc in last 6 dc: 93 dc.

Row 14: Ch 3, turn; dc in next 6 dc, 2 dc in next dc, (dc in next 12 dc, 2 dc in next dc) across to last 7 dc, dc in last 7 dc: 100 dc.

Row 15: Ch 3, turn; 2 dc in next dc, (dc in next 13 dc, 2 dc in next dc) across to last 14 dc, dc in last 14 dc: 107 dc.

Row 16: Ch 3, turn; 2 dc in next dc, (dc in next 14 dc, 2 dc in next dc) across to last 15 dc, dc in last 15 dc: 114 dc.

Row 17: Ch 3, turn; 2 dc in next dc, (dc in next 15 dc, 2 dc in next dc) across to last 16 dc, dc in last 16 dc: 121 dc.

Row 18: Ch 3, turn; 2 dc in next dc, (dc in next 16 dc, 2 dc in next dc) across to last 17 dc, dc in last 17 dc: 128 dc.

Row 19: Ch 3, turn; 2 dc in next dc, (dc in next 17 dc, 2 dc in next dc) across to last 18 dc, dc in last 18 dc: 135 dc.

Row 20: Ch 3, turn; 2 dc in next dc, (dc in next 18 dc, 2 dc in next dc) across to last 19 dc, dc in last 19 dc; finish off: 142 dc.

RUFFLE

Row 1: With **wrong** sides of Waffle Cone and Scoop together, Waffle Cone facing, and working through **both** layers, join Variegated with sc in first dc *(see Joining With Sc, page 42)*; sc in each st across: 73 sc.

Row 2: Ch 3, turn; dc in next 3 sc, 2 dc in next sc, (dc in next sc, 2 dc in next sc) across to last 2 sc, dc in last 2 sc: 107 dc.

Trim: Ch 1, do **not** turn; working in dc on Row 20 of Scoop, sc in first dc, ★ skip next dc, (hdc, 2 dc, hdc) in next dc, skip next dc, sc in next dc; repeat from ★ 34 times **more**, skip last dc, ch 3; working in dc on Row 2 of Ruffle, dc in first dc, † skip next dc, 5 dc in next dc, ch 1, skip next dc, sc in next dc, ch 1 †; repeat from † to † across to last 2 dc, skip next dc, 2 dc in last dc, ch 3; join with slip st to first sc, finish off.

With **wrong** sides together, working in ends of rows on **both** pieces, whipstitch Waffle Cone together *(Fig. 7b, page 45)*.

Mermaid Tail

EASY +

Finished Size: 52½" circumference at top edge x 42" long (133.5 cm x 106.5 cm) excluding Fins

SHOPPING LIST

Yarn (Jumbo Weight)

JUMBO 7

[7 ounces, 89 yards (200 grams, 81 meters) per skein]:

- ☐ 7 skeins

Crochet Hooks

- ☐ Size N/9 (10 mm) **and**
- ☐ Size P/Q (15 mm)

or sizes needed for gauge

Additional Supplies

- ☐ Yarn needle

GAUGE INFORMATION

With larger size hook, in pattern, 4 sts and 4 rows (one repeat) = 3½" (9 cm)

Gauge Swatch: 3½" (9 cm)
With larger size hook, ch 5.
Work same as Body for 4 rows: 4 sc.
Finish off.

STITCH GUIDE

SINGLE CROCHET 2 TOGETHER ***(abbreviated sc2tog)***
Pull up a loop in each of next 2 sc, YO and draw through all 3 loops on hook **(counts as one sc)**.

HALF DOUBLE CROCHET 2 TOGETHER ***(abbreviated hdc2tog)*** (uses next 2 sc)
★ YO, insert hook in **next** sc, YO and pull up a loop; repeat from ★ once **more**, YO and draw through all 5 loops on hook **(counts as one hdc)**.

BODY

With larger size hook, ch 61.

Row 1 (Right side)**:** Sc in second ch from hook and in each ch across: 60 sc.

Note: Loop a short piece of yarn around any stitch to mark Row 1 as **right** side.

Row 2: Ch 1, turn; sc in each sc across.

Row 3: Ch 1, turn; hdc in each sc across.

Rows 4-6: Ch 1, turn; sc in each st across.

Rows 7-22: Repeat Rows 3-6, 4 times.

SHAPING

Row 1: Ch 1, turn; (hdc in next 8 sc, hdc2tog) across: 54 hdc.

Rows 2-4: Ch 1, turn; sc in each st across.

Row 5: Ch 1, turn; hdc in each sc across.

Row 6: Ch 1, turn; sc in each hdc across.

Row 7: Ch 1, turn; (sc2tog, sc in next 7 sc) across: 48 sc.

Row 8: Ch 1, turn; sc in each sc across.

Row 9: Ch 1, turn; hdc in each sc across.

Rows 10-12: Ch 1, turn; sc in each st across.

Row 13: Ch 1, turn; (hdc in next 4 sc, hdc2tog) across: 40 hdc.

Rows 14-16: Ch 1, turn; sc in each st across.

Row 17: Ch 1, turn; (hdc2tog, hdc in next 3 sc) across: 32 hdc.

Rows 18-20: Ch 1, turn; sc in each st across.

Row 21: Ch 1, turn; (hdc in next 14 sc, hdc2tog) across: 30 hdc.

Rows 22-25: Ch 1, turn; sc in each st across.

Finish off leaving a long end for sewing.

Whipstitch center back seam *(Fig. 7b, page 45)*.

Flatten bottom edge having seam at center back, working in free loops of beginning ch ***(Fig. 3, page 44)***, whipstitch bottom seam ***(Fig. 7a, page 45)***.

FIN (Make 2)

With smaller size hook, ch 37.

Row 1 (Right side)**:** Sc in third ch from hook and in each ch across: 36 sc.

Note: Mark Row 1 as **right** side.

Row 2: Ch 1, turn; sc in Back Loop Only of each sc across to last 3 sc ***(Fig. 2, page 44)***, leave remaining sts unworked: 33 sc.

Row 3: Ch 1, turn; sc in Back Loop Only of each sc across.

Rows 4-13: Repeat Rows 2 and 3, 5 times: 18 sc.

Finish off leaving a long for sewing on one Fin only.

With **wrong** sides together, matching sc on Row 13, and working through **both** loops of each stitch on **both** pieces, whipstitch Fins together leaving last 3 sts unsewn.

Trim: With **right** side facing and using smaller size hook, join yarn with sc in end of first row ***(see Joining With Sc, page 42)***; work 15 sc evenly spaced across ends of rows; finish off leaving a long end for sewing.

Using long end, sew Fins to bottom edge of Body.

Pencils

EASY +

Finished Size: 50" circumference at top edge x 50" long (127 cm x 127 cm) excluding Points

SHOPPING LIST

Yarn (Medium Weight) MEDIUM 4

[7 ounces, 364 yards (198 grams, 333 meters) per skein]:

- ☐ Yellow - 6 skeins
- ☐ Blue - 2 skeins
- ☐ Orange - 2 skeins
- ☐ Green - 2 skeins
- ☐ Aran - 1 skein

Crochet Hook

- ☐ Size L (8 mm) **or** size needed for gauge

Additional Supplies

- ☐ Yarn needle

Hold two strands of yarn together throughout.

GAUGE INFORMATION

In pattern,
10 sts and 6 rows = 4" (10 cm)

Gauge Swatch: 8½" wide x 4" high (21.5 cm x 10 cm)

Work same as Body on page 22 for 6 rows: 21 sts.

STITCH GUIDE

FRONT POST DOUBLE CROCHET *(abbreviated FPdc)*

YO, insert hook from **front** to **back** around post of st indicated ***(Fig. 4, page 44)***, YO and pull up a loop (3 loops on hook), (YO and draw through 2 loops on hook) twice.

BACK POST DOUBLE CROCHET *(abbreviated BPdc)*

YO, insert hook from **back** to **front** around post of next st indicated ***(Fig. 4, page 44)***, YO and pull up a loop (3 loops on hook), (YO and draw through 2 loops on hook) twice.

SINGLE CROCHET 2 TOGETHER *(abbreviated sc2tog)*

Pull up a loop in each of next 2 sc, YO and draw through all 3 loops on hook **(counts as one sc)**.

SINGLE CROCHET 3 TOGETHER *(abbreviated sc3tog)*

Pull up a loop in each of next 3 sc, YO and draw through all 4 loops on hook **(counts as one sc)**.

STRIP (Make 3 of Yellow and one **each** of Blue, Orange, and Green)

BODY

With color indicated, ch 23.

Row 1: Dc in fourth ch from hook and in each ch across **(3 skipped chs count as first dc)**: 21 dc.

Row 2 (Right side)**:** Ch 3 **(counts as first dc, now and throughout)**, turn; dc in next 3 dc, work FPdc around next dc, (dc in next 5 dc, work FPdc around next dc) twice, dc in last 4 dc.

Note: Loop a short piece of yarn around any stitch to mark Row 2 as **right** side.

Row 3: Ch 3, turn; dc in next 3 dc, work BPdc around next FPdc, (dc in next 5 dc, work BPdc around next FPdc) twice, dc in last 4 dc.

Row 4: Ch 3, turn; dc in next 3 dc, work FPdc around next BPdc, (dc in next 5 dc, work FPdc around next BPdc) twice, dc in last 4 dc.

Repeat Rows 3 and 4 until piece measures approximately 50" (127 cm) from beginning ch, ending by working Row 4.

Finish off.

POINT

Row 1: With **right** side facing, join Aran with slip st in first dc; ch 1, skip first dc, sc in next dc and in each st across: 20 sc.

Row 2: Ch 1, turn; skip first sc, sc in each sc across: 19 sc.

Rows 3-8: Ch 1, turn; skip first sc, sc in each sc across to last 2 sc, sc2tog: 7 sc.

Finish off.

Row 9: With **right** side facing, join same color as Body with sc in first sc ***(see Joining With Sc, page 42)***; sc in each sc across: 7 sc.

Row 10: Ch 1, turn; skip first sc, sc in next 4 sc, sc2tog: 5 sc.

Row 11: Ch 1, turn; skip first sc, sc in next 2 sc, sc2tog: 3 sc.

Row 12: Ch 1, turn; sc3tog; finish off.

Join Strips in following order: Green, Yellow, Orange, Yellow, Blue, and Yellow.

With **wrong** sides of two Strips together, whipstitch across long edge of Body ***(Fig. 7b, page 45)***. Repeat with remaining Strips.

Whipstitch first Strip to last Strip to form a tube.

Flatten piece with 3 Strips for front and back. Working in free loops of beginning chs ***(Fig. 3, page 44)***, whipstitch bottom edge closed ***(Fig. 7a, page 45)***.

Pizza Slice

EASY

Finished Size: 56" circumference at top edge x 46" long (142 cm x 117 cm)

SHOPPING LIST

Yarn (Medium Weight) MEDIUM 4

[16 ounces, 812 yards (453 grams, 742 meters) per skein**]:**

- ☐ Brown - 4 skeins
- ☐ Yellow - 2 skeins

[6 ounces, 315 yards (170 grams, 288 meters) per skein**]:**

- ☐ Red - 1 skein
- ☐ Off White - 90 yards (83 meters)

Crochet Hooks

- ☐ Size M (13 mm) **or** sizes needed for gauge
- ☐ Size H (5 mm) (for joining only)

Additional Supplies

- ☐ Yarn needle

GAUGE INFORMATION

With larger hook and holding two strands of yarn together,
8 hdc and 6 rows = 4" (10 cm)

Gauge Swatch: 4" (10 cm) square

With larger hook, ch 9.

Row 1: Hdc in third ch from hook and in each ch across **(2 skipped chs count as first hdc)**: 8 hdc.

Rows 2-6: Ch 2 **(counts as first hdc)**, turn; hdc in next hdc and in each hdc across.

Finish off.

STITCH GUIDE

TREBLE CROCHET ***(abbreviated tr)***

YO twice, insert hook in st or sp indicated, YO and pull up a loop (4 loops on hook), (YO and draw through 2 loops on hook) 3 times.

FRONT

With two strands of Yellow held together and larger size hook, ch 3.

Row 1 (Right side)**:** 2 Hdc in third ch from hook **(2 skipped chs count as first hdc)**: 3 hdc.

Note: Loop a short piece of yarn around any stitch to mark Row 1 as **right** side.

Row 2: Ch 2, turn; hdc in first hdc, hdc in next hdc, 2 hdc in last hdc: 5 hdc.

Rows 3-52: Ch 2, turn; hdc in first hdc and in each hdc across: 55 hdc.

Rows 52-60: Ch 2, turn; hdc in next hdc and in each hdc across.

Row 61: Ch 3 **(counts as first dc, now and throughout)**, turn; hdc in next hdc, sc in next hdc, slip st in next hdc, sc in next hdc, hdc in next hdc, dc in next hdc, ★ tr in next hdc, dc in next hdc, hdc in next hdc, sc in next hdc, slip st in next hdc, sc in next hdc, hdc in next hdc, dc in next hdc; repeat from ★ across; finish off.

Row 62: With **right** side facing, holding three strands of Red together, and using larger size hook, join yarn with sc in first dc ***(see Joining With Sc, page 42)***; hdc in next hdc, dc in next sc, tr in next slip st, dc in next sc, hdc in next hdc, sc in next dc, ★ slip st in next tr, sc in next dc, dc in next sc, tr in next slip st, dc in next sc, hdc in next hdc, sc in next dc; repeat from ★ across.

Row 63: Ch 2, turn; (hdc in next 4 sts, dc in next 5 sts) across to last 5 sts, hdc in last 5 sts.

Row 64: Ch 2, turn; hdc in next hdc and in each st across; finish off.

Row 65: With **wrong** side facing, holding two strands of Brown together, and using larger size hook, join yarn with hdc in first hdc ***(see Joining With Hdc, page 42)***; hdc in each st across.

Rows 66-68: Ch 2, turn; hdc in next hdc and in each hdc across.

Finish off.

PEPPERONI (Make 8)

Rnd 1 (Right side)**:** Holding two strands of Red together and using larger size hook, make an adjustable loop to form a ring; ch 3, 11 dc in ring; join with slip st to first dc: 12 dc.

Rnd 2: Ch 1, 2 sc in each dc around; join with slip st to first sc, finish off leaving a long end for sewing.

MUSHROOM (Make 4)

Top (Right side)**:** Holding two strands of Off White together and using larger size hook, make an adjustable loop to form a ring; ch 4, (8 tr, ch 4, slip st) in ring; do **not** join.

Stem: Ch 6, sc in second ch from hook and in next 4 chs, slip st in ring; finish off leaving a long end for sewing.

Using photo as a guide for placement and long ends, sew Pepperonis and Mushrooms to Front.

BACK

Holding two strands of Brown together and using larger size hook, work same as Front through Row 52: 55 hdc.

Rows 53-68: Ch 2, turn; hdc in next hdc and in each hdc across.

Finish off.

JOINING

Place Front and Back with **wrong** sides together and Front facing. With smaller size hook and working through **both** pieces, join one strand of Brown with sc in end of Row 68; sc evenly across ends of rows to beginning ring; 3 sc in ring; sc evenly across ends of rows; finish off.

Watermelon Slice

EASY **Finished Size:** 68" in circumference at top edge x 45" long (172.5 cm x 114.5 cm)

SHOPPING LIST

Yarn (Medium Weight) 4 MEDIUM

[3.5 ounces, 170 yards (100 grams, 156 meters) per skein]:

- ☐ Red - 8 skeins
- ☐ Green - 1 skein
- ☐ White - 50 yards (46 meters)
- ☐ Light Green - 20 yards (18.5 meters)
- ☐ Black - 15 yards (13.5 meters)

Crochet Hook

- ☐ Size K (6 mm) **or** size needed for gauge

Additional Supplies

- ☐ Yarn needle

GAUGE INFORMATION

12 dc and 8 rows = 4" (10 cm)

Gauge Swatch: 4" (10 cm) square

With larger hook, ch 14.

Row 1: Dc in fourth ch from hook and in each ch across **(3 skipped chs count as first dc)**: 12 dc.

Rows 2-8: Ch 3 **(counts as first dc)**, turn; dc in next dc and in each dc across.

Finish off.

STITCH GUIDE

PUFF STITCH ***(abbreviated Puff St)***

(uses one st or sp)

★ YO, insert hook in st or sp indicated, YO and pull up a loop even with loop on hook; repeat from ★ 2 times **more**, YO and draw through all 7 loops on hook.

FRONT

With Red, ch 4; join with slip st to form a ring.

Row 1: Ch 3 **(counts as first dc, now and throughout)**, work Puff St, (ch 1, work Puff St in ring) twice; do **not** join: 3 Puff Sts, one dc, and 2 ch-1 sps.

Row 2 (Right side)**:** Ch 3, turn; work Puff St in first Puff St, 3 dc in each of next 2 ch-1 sps, skip next Puff St, work Puff St in last dc: 7 dc and 2 Puff Sts.

Note: Loop a short piece of yarn around any stitch to mark Row 2 as **right** side.

IZZE

Row 3: Ch 3, turn; work Puff St in first Puff St, 2 dc in next dc, dc in next 4 dc, 2 dc in next dc, skip next Puff St, work Puff St in last dc: 9 dc and 2 Puff Sts.

Rows 4 and 5: Ch 3, turn; work Puff St in first Puff St, 2 dc in next dc, dc in next dc and in each dc across to last 3 sts, 2 dc in next dc, skip next Puff St, work Puff St in last dc: 13 dc and 2 Puff Sts.

Row 6: Ch 3, turn; work Puff St in first Puff St, dc in next dc and in each dc across to last Puff St, skip last Puff St, work Puff St in last dc.

Rows 7-63: Repeat Rows 4-6, 19 times: 89 dc and 2 Puff Sts.

Rows 64-72: Repeat Row 4, 9 times: 107 dc and 2 Puff Sts.

Rows 73-79: Repeat Row 6, 7 times; finish off.

Row 80: With **right** side facing, join White with slip st in first Puff St; ch 3, work Puff St in same st, dc in next dc and in each dc across to last 2 sts, skip next Puff St, work Puff St in last dc.

Rows 81 and 82: Repeat Row 6 twice.

Finish off.

Row 83: With Light Green, repeat Row 80; finish off.

Row 84: With Green, repeat Row 80.

Rows 85-87: Repeat Row 6, 3 times.

Row 88: Ch 3, turn; work Puff St in first Puff St, skip next dc, sc in next dc, ★ skip next dc, 5 dc in next dc, skip next dc, sc in next dc; repeat from ★ across to last 2 sts, skip next Puff St, work Puff St in last dc; finish off.

Using photo as a guide for placement, using satin stitch ***(Fig. 9, page 46)*** and Black, add seeds around post of dc.

BACK

With Red, ch 4; join with slip st to form a ring.

Row 1 (Right side)**:** Ch 3, work Puff St, (ch 1, work Puff St in ring) twice; do **not** join: 3 Puff Sts, one dc, and 2 ch-1 sps.

Row 2: Ch 3, turn; 3 dc in each of next 2 ch-1 sps, dc in last dc: 8 dc.

Rows 3-5: Ch 3, turn; dc in first dc and in next dc and each dc across to last dc, 2 dc in last dc: 14 dc.

Row 6: Ch 3, turn; dc in next dc and in each dc across.

Rows 7 and 8: Ch 3, turn; dc in first dc and in next dc and each dc across across to last dc, 2 dc in last dc: 18 dc.

Rows 9-60: Repeat Rows 6-8, 17 times; then repeat Row 6 once **more**: 86 dc.

Rows 61-71: Ch 3, turn; dc in first dc and in next dc and each dc across across to last dc, 2 dc in last dc: 108 dc.

Rows 72-86: Ch 3, turn; dc in next dc and in each dc across.

Finish off.

Row 87: With **right** side facing, join Green with sc in first dc; ★ skip next dc, sc in next dc, skip next dc, 5 dc in next dc; repeat from ★ across to last 3 dc, skip next dc, sc in last 2 dc; finish off.

With **wrong** sides together, sew dc on ends of rows on Back to second and next-to-last dc on rows of Front (inside edge of Puff Sts).

Sugar Skull

EASY +

Finished Size:
39" at widest point x 46" long (99 cm x 117 cm)

SHOPPING LIST

Yarn (Bulky Weight)

BULKY 5

[3.5 ounces, 109 yards (100 grams, 100 meters) per skein**]**:

- ☐ White - 20 skeins
- ☐ Black - 2 skeins
- ☐ Variegated - 80 yards (73 meters)
- ☐ Green - 45 yards (41meters)
- ☐ Blue - 40 yards (36.5 meters)

Crochet Hook

- ☐ Size L (8 mm) **or** size needed for gauge

Additional Supplies

- ☐ Yarn needle

GAUGE INFORMATION

10 dc and 8 rows = 4" (10 cm)

Gauge Swatch: 4" (10 cm) square

With larger hook, ch 12.

Row 1: Dc in fourth ch from hook and in each ch across **(3 skipped chs count as first dc)**: 10 dc.

Row 2: Ch 1, turn; sc in each dc across.

Row 3: Ch 3 **(counts as first dc)**, turn; dc in next sc and in each sc across.

Rows 4-8: Repeat Rows 2 and 3 twice, then repeat Row 2 once **more**.

Finish off.

STITCH GUIDE

TREBLE CROCHET *(abbreviated tr)*
YO twice, insert hook in st indicated, YO and pull up a loop (4 loops on hook), (YO and draw through 2 loops on hook) 3 times.

SINGLE CROCHET 2 TOGETHER *(abbreviated sc2tog)*
Pull up a loop in each of next 2 dc, YO and draw through all 3 loops on hook **(counts as one sc)**.

SINGLE CROCHET 3 TOGETHER *(abbreviated sc3tog)*
Pull up a loop in each of next 3 dc, YO and draw through all 4 loops on hook **(counts as one sc)**.

DOUBLE CROCHET 2 TOGETHER *(abbreviated dc2tog)*
(uses next 2 sc)
★ YO, insert hook in **next** sc, YO and pull up a loop, YO and draw through 2 loops on hook; repeat from ★ once **more**, YO and draw through all 3 loops on hook **(counts as one dc)**.

DOUBLE CROCHET 3 TOGETHER *(abbreviated dc3tog)*
(uses next 3 sc)
★ YO, insert hook in **next** sc, YO and pull up a loop, YO and draw through 2 loops on hook; repeat from ★ 2 times **more**, YO and draw through all 4 loops on hook **(counts as one dc)**.

BODY (Make 2)

With White, ch 39.

Row 1 (Right side)**:** Sc in second ch from hook and in each ch across: 38 sc.

Note: Loop a short piece of yarn around any stitch to mark Row 1 as **right** side.

Row 2: Ch 3 **(counts as first dc, now and throughout)**, turn; 2 dc in first sc, dc in next sc and in each sc across to last sc, 3 dc in last sc: 42 dc.

Row 3: Ch 1, turn; 2 sc in each of next 2 dc, sc in each dc across to last 2 dc, 2 sc in each of last 2 dc: 46 sc.

Row 4: Ch 3, turn; dc in first sc and in next sc and each sc across to last sc, 2 dc in last sc: 48 dc.

Row 5 (Increase row)**:** Ch 1, 2 sc in first dc, sc in each dc across to last dc, 2 sc in last dc: 50 sc.

Row 6 (Increase row)**:** Ch 3, turn; dc in first sc and in next sc and each across to last sc, 2 dc in last sc: 52 dc.

Row 7: Ch 1, turn; sc in each dc across.

Rows 8-13: Repeat Rows 6 and 7, 3 times: 58 sc.

Row 14: Ch 3, turn; dc in next sc and in each sc across.

Row 15: Repeat Row 5: 60 sc.

Row 16: Ch 3, turn; dc in next sc and in each sc across.

Row 17: Ch 1, turn; sc in each dc across.

Row 18: Repeat Row 6: 62 dc.

Row 19: Ch 1, turn; sc in each dc across.

Row 20: Ch 3, turn; dc in next sc and in each sc across.

Rows 21 and 22: Repeat Rows 19 and 20.

Row 23: Repeat Row 5: 64 sc.

Row 24: Ch 3, turn; dc in next sc and in each sc across.

Rows 25-27: Repeat Rows 5 and 6 once, then repeat Row 5 once more: 70 sc.

Row 28: Ch 3, turn; dc in next sc and in each sc across.

Rows 29-31: Repeat Rows 5 and 6 once, then repeat Row 5 once more: 76 sc.

Row 32: Ch 3, turn; dc in next sc and in each sc across.

Row 33: Repeat Row 5: 78 sc.

Row 34: Ch 3, turn; dc in next sc and in each sc across.

Rows 35-42: Repeat Rows 19 and 20, 4 times.

Row 43: Repeat Row 5: 80 sc.

Row 44: Ch 3, turn; dc in next sc and in each sc across.

Rows 45-48: Repeat Rows 5 and 6 twice: 84 dc.

Row 49: Repeat Row 19.

Row 50: Repeat Row 6: 86 dc.

Rows 51-53: Repeat Rows 19 and 20 once, then repeat Row 19 once more.

Row 54: Repeat Row 6: 88 dc.

Rows 55 and 56: Repeat Rows 19 and 20.

Row 57: Repeat Row 5: 90 sc.

Row 58: Ch 3, turn; dc in next sc and in each sc across.

Row 59: Ch 1, turn; sc in each dc across.

Rows 60-71: Repeat Rows 58 and 59, 6 times.

Row 72 (Decrease row)**:** Ch 3, turn; dc2tog, dc in next sc and in each sc across to last 2 sc, dc2tog: 88 dc.

Row 73: Ch 1, turn; sc in each dc across, place marker in first and last sc for joining.

Rows 74-78: Repeat Rows 72 and 73 twice, then repeat Row 72 once **more**: 82 sc.

Row 79 (Decrease row)**:** Ch 1, turn; sc2tog, sc in each dc across to last 2 dc, sc2tog: 80 sc.

Row 80: Ch 3, turn; dc in next sc and in each sc across.

Row 81: Repeat Row 79: 78 sc.

Row 82: Ch 3, turn; dc in next sc and in each sc across.

Row 83 (Decrease row)**:** Ch 1, turn; sc2tog, sc in each dc across to last 2 dc, sc2tog: 76 sc.

Row 84 (Decrease row)**:** Ch 3, turn; dc2tog, dc in next sc and in each sc across to last 2 sc, dc2tog: 74 dc.

Rows 85-92: Repeat Rows 83 and 84, 4 times: 58 dc.

Row 93 (Decrease row)**:** Ch 1, turn; sc3tog, sc in each dc across to last 3 dc, sc3tog: 54 sc.

Row 94: Repeat Row 84: 52 dc.

Row 95: Repeat Row 93: 48 sc.

Row 96: Ch 3, turn; dc3tog, dc in next sc and in each sc across to last 3 sc, dc3tog: 44 dc.

Row 97: Turn; slip st in first 4 dc, ch 1, sc in each dc across to last 4 dc, leave last 4 dc unworked: 36 sc.

Row 98: Turn; slip st in first 6 sc, ch 3, dc in next sc and in each sc across to last 5 sc, leave last 5 sc unworked: 26 dc.

Trim: Ch 1, turn; sc evenly around entire Body; join with slip st to first sc, finish off.

EYE (Make 2)

Rnd 1 (Right side)**:** With Blue, make an adjustable loop to form a ring ***(Figs. 1a-d, page 43)***; ch 3, dc in ring, ch 1, (2 dc in ring, ch 1) 5 times; join with slip st to first dc, finish off: 12 dc and 6 ch-1 sps.

Note: Mark Rnd 1 as **right** side.

Rnd 2: With **right** side facing, join Variegated with dc in any ch-1 sp ***(see Joining With Dc, page 42)***; (dc, ch 3, 2 dc) in same sp, (2 dc, ch 3, 2 dc) in each of next 5 ch-1 sps; join with slip st to first dc: 24 dc and 6 ch-3 sps.

Rnd 3: Slip st in next dc and in next ch-3 sp, ch 3, 7 dc in same sp, skip next 2 dc, slip st in sp **before** next dc ***(Fig. 6, page 45)***, ★ 8 dc in next ch-3 sp, skip next 2 dc, slip st in sp **before** next dc; repeat from ★ around; join with slip st to first dc, finish off: 48 dc and 6 slip sts.

Rnd 4: With **right** side facing, join Green with sc in first dc of any 8-dc group ***(see Joining With Sc, page 42)***; sc in next 3 dc, ch 1, sc in next 4 dc, working **around** slip st on Rnd 3 ***(Fig. 5, page 44)***, sc in same sp on Rnd 2 as slip st, ★ sc in next 4 dc, ch 1, sc in next 4 dc, working **around** slip st on Rnd 3, sc in same sp on Rnd 2 as slip st; repeat from ★ around; join with slip st to first sc, finish off: 54 sc and 6 ch-1 sps.

Rnd 5: With **right** side facing, join Black with sc in any ch-1 sp; 2 sc in same sp, skip next sc, 2 sc in next sc, skip next sc, dc in next 3 sc, skip next sc, 2 sc in next sc, skip next sc, ★ 3 sc in next ch-1 sp, skip next sc, 2 sc in next sc, skip next sc, dc in next 3 sc, skip next sc, 2 sc in next sc, skip next sc; repeat from ★ around; join with slip st to first sc: 60 sts.

Rnd 6: Ch 3, dc in same st as joining and in next 9 sts, (2 dc in next sc, dc in next 9 sts) around; join with slip st to first dc: 66 dc.

Rnd 7: Ch 3, dc in same st as joining and in next 10 dc, (2 dc in next dc, dc in next 10 dc) around; join with slip st to first dc, finish off leaving a long end for sewing: 72 dc.

NOSE

Rnd 1 (Right side)**:** With Variegated, make an adjustable loop to form a ring, ch 2 (**counts as first hdc, now and throughout**), 11 dc in ring; join with slip st to first hdc: 12 sts.

Note: Mark Rnd 1 as **right** side.

Rnd 2: Ch 2, 2 dc in each of next 11 dc; join with slip st to first hdc: 23 sts.

Rnd 3: Ch 2, 2 dc in next dc, (dc in next dc, 2 dc in next dc) 5 times, 3 dc in next dc, (dc in next dc, 2 dc in next dc) 5 times; join with slip st to first hdc: 36 sts.

Rnd 4: Sc in next dc, (dc, hdc) in next dc, 2 dc in each of next 5 dc, dc in next 2 dc, hdc in next 2 dc, sc in next 4 dc, hdc in next dc, dc in next dc, 3 dc in next dc, dc in next dc, hdc in next dc, sc in next 4 dc, hdc in next 2 dc, dc in next 2 dc, 2 dc in each of next 5 dc, (dc, hdc) in next dc, sc in last dc; join with slip st to joining slip st, finish off leaving a long end for sewing.

LONG LEAF

With Green, ch 25.

Rnd 1 (Right side)**:** Sc in third ch from hook **(2 skipped chs count as first ch-2 sp)** and in next 5 chs, hdc in next 8 chs, dc in next 8 chs, 8 tr in last ch; working in free loops of beginning ch ***(Fig. 3, page 44)***, dc in next 8 chs, hdc in next 8 chs, sc in next 6 chs, slip st in first ch-2 sp, finish off leaving a long end for sewing.

SHORT LEAF (Make 2)

With Green, ch 13.

Rnd 1 (Right side)**:** Sc in third ch from hook **(2 skipped chs count as first ch-2 sp)** and in next 2 chs, hdc in next 3 chs, dc in next 4 chs, 8 dc in last ch; working in free loops of beginning ch, dc in next 4 chs, hdc in next 3 chs, sc in next 3 chs, slip st in first ch-2 sp, finish off leaving a long end for sewing.

LARGE FLOWER (Make 2)

Rnd 1 (Right side)**:** With White, make an adjustable loop to form a ring, ch 3, 11 dc in ring; join with slip st to first dc; finish off leaving a long end for sewing: 12 dc.

Note: Mark Rnd 1 as **right** side.

Rnd 2: With **right** side facing, join Blue with sc in any dc; (hdc, dc, 2 tr, dc, hdc, sc) in same st, skip next dc, ★ (sc, hdc, dc, 2 tr, dc, hdc, sc) in next dc, skip next dc; repeat from ★ around; join with slip st to first sc, finish off leaving a long end for sewing.

SMALL FLOWER
(Make 3)

Rnd 1 (Right side)**:** With Variegated, make an adjustable loop to form a ring, ch 1, ★ (sc, ch 2, tr) in ring, ch 2; repeat from ★ 4 times **more**; join with slip st to first sc, finish off leaving a long end for sewing.

MOUTH

With Black, ch 33.

Rnd 1 (Right side)**:** 4 Dc in fourth ch from hook **(3 skipped chs count as first dc)**, dc in each ch across to last ch, 5 dc in last ch; dc in free loops of each ch across; join with slip st to first dc: 66 dc.

Note: Mark Rnd 1 as **right** side.

Rnd 2: Ch 3, dc in same st as joining, 2 dc in each of next 5 dc, dc in next 26 dc, 2 dc in each of next 7 dc, dc in next 26 dc, 2 dc in last dc; join with slip st to first dc, finish off: 80 dc.

Rnd 3: With **right** side facing, join White with slip st in any dc; slip st in each dc around; join with slip st to joining slip st, finish off leaving a long end for sewing.

Using photo as a guide for placement, with White and using running stitch ***(Fig. 10, page 46)***, add center line to Mouth; with straight stitch ***(Fig. 8, page 46)*** and White, add teeth to Mouth.

Using photo as a guide for placement and long ends, sew Eyes, Nose, Mouth, Leaves, and Flowers to front.

With **wrong** sides together, working through **both** loops of each stitch on **both** pieces, beginning and ending in marked sc, whipstitch pieces together ***(Fig. 7a, page 45)***.

General Instructions

ABBREVIATIONS

BPdc	Back Post double crochet(s)
ch(s)	chain(s)
cm	centimeters
dc	double crochet(s)
dc2tog	double crochet 2 together
dc3tog	double crochet 3 together
FPdc	Front Post double crochet(s)
hdc	half double crochet(s)
hdc2tog	half double crochet 2 together
mm	millimeters
Rnd(s)	Round(s)
sc	single crochet(s)
sc2tog	single crochet 2 together
sc3tog	single crochet 3 together
sp(s)	space(s)
st(s)	stitch(es)
tr	treble crochet(s)
YO	yarn over

SYMBOLS & TERMS

★ — work instructions following ★ as many **more** times as indicated in addition to the first time.

† to † — work all instructions from first † to second † **as many** times as specified.

( ) or **[ ]** — work enclosed instructions **as many** times as specified by the number immediately following **or** work all enclosed instructions in the stitch or space indicated **or** contains explanatory remarks.

colon (:) — the number(s) given after a colon at the end of a row or round denote(s) the number of stitches or spaces you should have on that row or round.

Yarn Weight Symbol & Names	LACE 0	SUPER FINE 1	FINE 2	LIGHT 3	MEDIUM 4	BULKY 5	SUPER BULKY 6	JUMBO 7
Type of Yarns in Category	Fingering, size 10 crochet thread	Sock, Fingering, Baby	Sport, Baby	DK, Light Worsted	Worsted, Afghan, Aran	Chunky, Craft, Rug	Super Bulky, Roving	Jumbo, Roving
Crochet Gauge* Ranges in Single Crochet to 4" (10 cm)	32-42 sts**	21-32 sts	16-20 sts	12-17 sts	11-14 sts	8-11 sts	6-9 sts	5 sts and fewer
Advised Hook Size Range	Steel*** 6 to 8, Regular hook B-1	B-1 to E-4	E-4 to 7	7 to I-9	I-9 to K-10½	K-10½ to M/N-13	M/N-13 to Q	Q and larger

*GUIDELINES ONLY: The chart above reflects the most commonly used gauges and hook sizes for specific yarn categories.

** Lace weight yarns are usually crocheted with larger hooks to create lacy openwork patterns. Accordingly, a gauge range is difficult to determine. Always follow the gauge stated in your pattern.

*** Steel crochet hooks are sized differently from regular hooks–the higher the number, the smaller the hook, which is the reverse of regular hook sizing.

GAUGE

Exact gauge is **essential** for proper size. Before beginning your project, make the sample swatch given in the individual instructions in the yarn and hook specified. After completing the swatch, measure it, counting your stitches and rows or rounds carefully. If your swatch is larger or smaller than specified, **make another, changing hook size to get the correct gauge**. Keep trying until you find the size hook that will give you the specified gauge.

CROCHET TERMINOLOGY		
UNITED STATES		INTERNATIONAL
slip stitch (slip st)	=	single crochet (sc)
single crochet (sc)	=	double crochet (dc)
half double crochet (hdc)	=	half treble crochet (htr)
double crochet (dc)	=	treble crochet (tr)
treble crochet (tr)	=	double treble crochet (dtr)
double treble crochet (dtr)	=	triple treble crochet (ttr)
triple treble crochet (tr tr)	=	quadruple treble crochet (qtr)
skip	=	miss

JOINING WITH SC

When instructed to join with sc, begin with a slip knot on hook. Insert hook in stitch indicated, YO and pull up a loop, YO and draw through both loops on hook.

JOINING WITH HDC

When instructed to join with hdc, begin with a slip knot on hook. YO, holding loop on hook, insert hook in stitch indicated, YO and pull up a loop (3 loops on hook), YO and draw through 3 loops on hook

JOINING WITH DC

When instructed to join with dc, begin with a slip knot on hook. YO, holding loop on hook, insert hook in stitch indicated, YO and pull up a loop (3 loops on hook), (YO and draw through 2 loops on hook) twice.

BEGINNER	Projects for first-time crocheters using basic stitches. Minimal shaping.
EASY	Projects using yarn with basic stitches, repetitive stitch patterns, simple color changes, and simple shaping and finishing.
INTERMEDIATE	Projects using a variety of techniques, such as basic lace patterns or color patterns, mid-level shaping and finishing.
EXPERIENCED	Projects with intricate stitch patterns, techniques and dimension, such as non-repeating patterns, multi-color techniques, fine threads, small hooks, detailed shaping and refined finishing.

ADJUSTABLE LOOP

Wind yarn around two fingers to form a ring *(Fig. 1a)*. Slide yarn off fingers and grasp the strands at the top of the ring *(Fig. 1b)*. Insert hook from **front** to **back** into the ring, pull up a loop, YO and draw through loop on hook to lock ring ***(Fig. 1c)*** (st made does **not** count as part of beginning ch). Working around both strands, follow instructions to work sts in the ring, then pull yarn tail to close *(Fig. 1d)*.

Fig. 1a

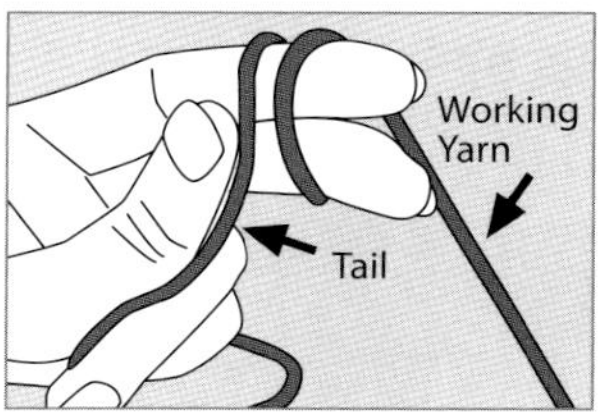

Fig. 1b

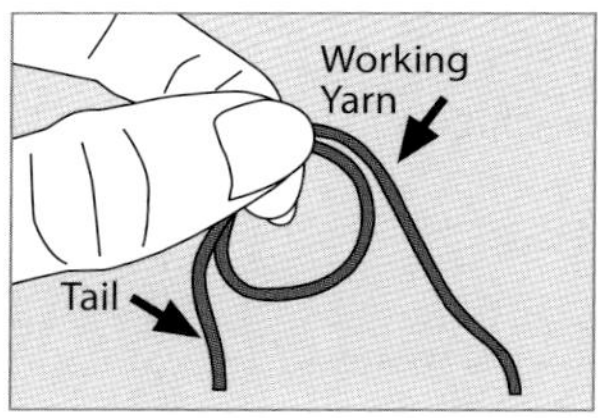

Fig. 1c

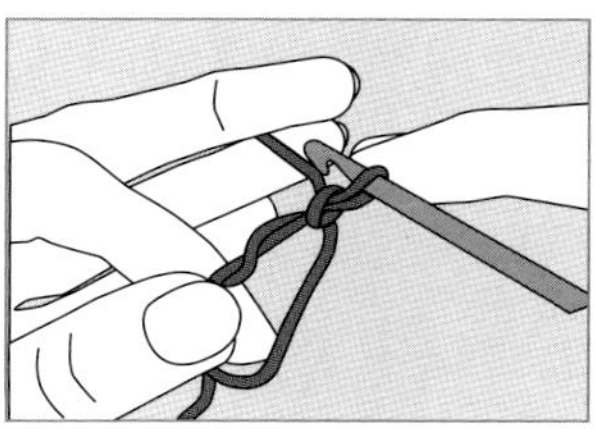

Fig. 1d

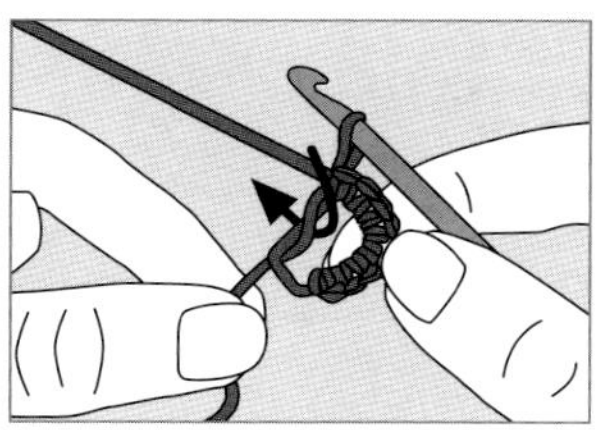

CROCHET HOOKS	
U.S.	**Metric mm**
B-1	2.25
C-2	2.75
D-3	3.25
E-4	3.5
F-5	3.75
G-6	4
7	4.5
H-8	5
I-9	5.5
J-10	6
K-10½	6.5
L-11	8
M/N-13	9
N/P-15	10
P/Q	15
Q	16
S	19

BACK LOOPS ONLY

Work only in loop(s) indicated by arrow *(Fig. 2)*.

Fig. 2

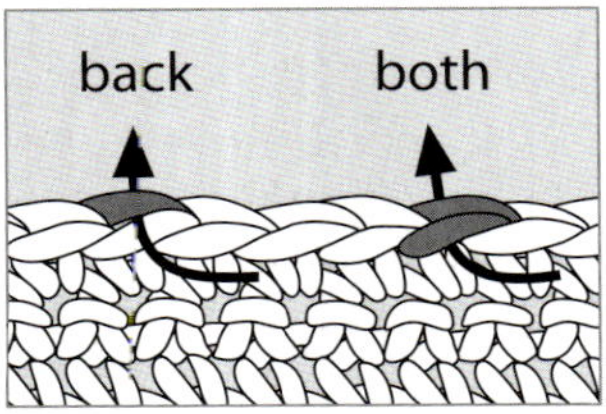

FREE LOOPS OF A CHAIN

When instructed to work in free loops of a chain, work in loop indicated by arrow *(Fig. 3)*.

Fig. 3

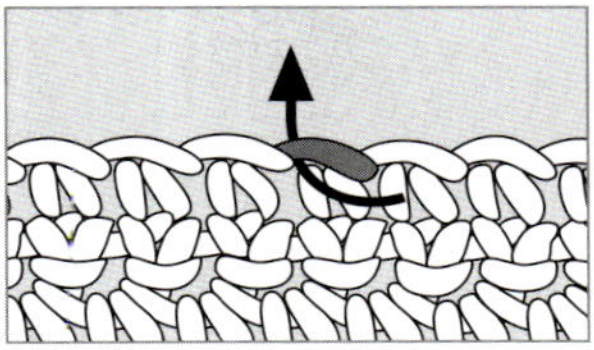

POST STITCH

Work around post of stitch indicated, inserting hook in direction of arrow *(Fig. 4)*.

Fig. 4

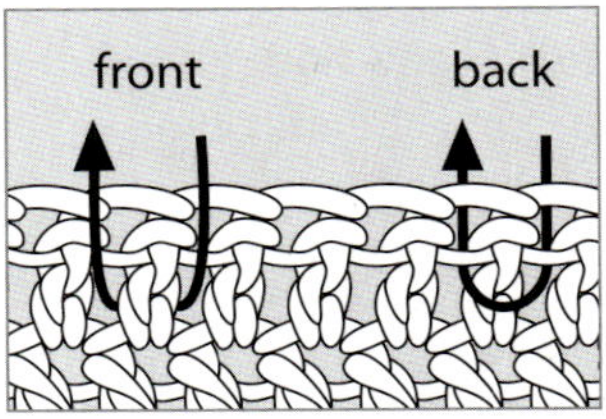

WORKING AROUND A STITCH

Work in stitch indicated, inserting hook in direction of arrow *(Fig. 5)*.

Fig. 5

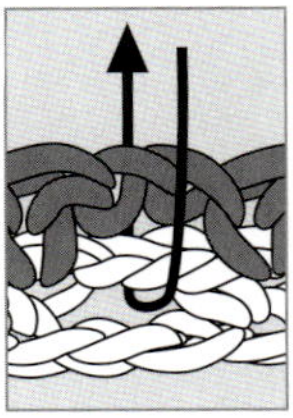

WORKING IN SPACE BEFORE A STITCH

When instructed to work in space **before** a stitch or in spaces **between** stitches, insert hook in space indicated by arrow ***(Fig. 6)***.

Fig. 6

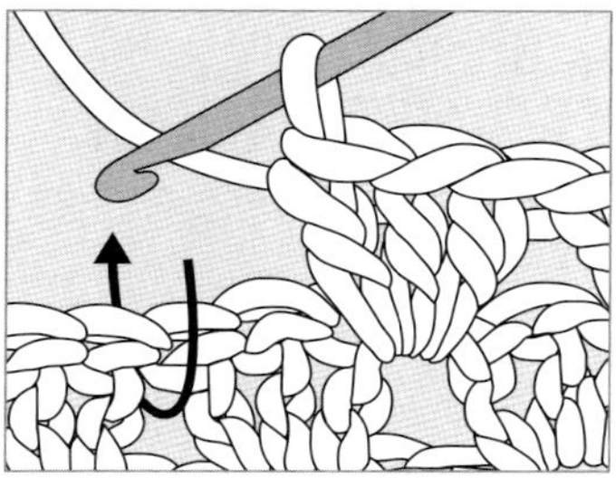

WHIPSTITCH

With **wrong** sides together, sew through both pieces once to secure the beginning of the seam, leaving an ample yarn end to weave in later. Insert the needle from **back** to **front** through two strands on each stitch of each piece ***(Fig. 7a)*** **or** through ends of rows ***(Fig. 7b)***. Bring the needle around and insert it from **back** to **front** through the next strands on both pieces.
Repeat along the edge, being careful to match stitches and rows.

Fig. 7a

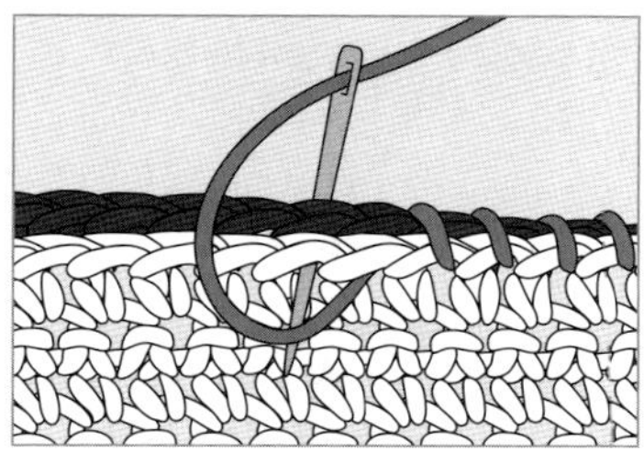

Fig. 7b

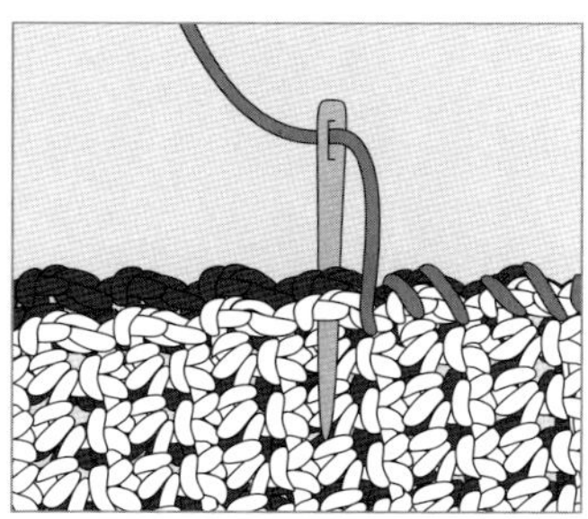

EMBROIDERY STITCHES

STRAIGHT STITCH

Straight stitch is just what the name implies, a single, straight stitch. Come up at 1 and go down at 2 ***(Fig. 8)***.

Fig. 8

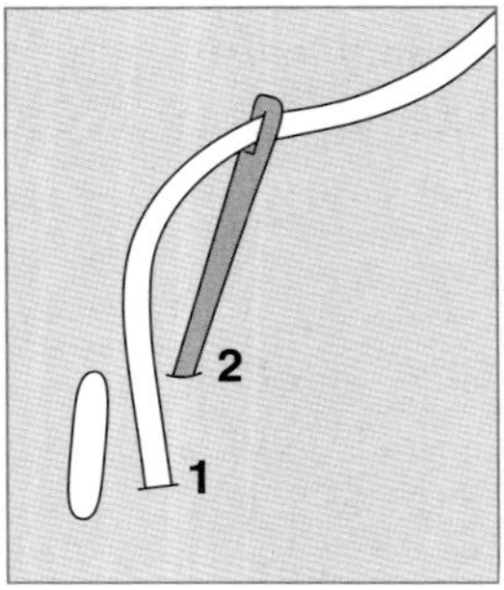

SATIN STITCH

Satin stitch is a series of straight stitches worked side by side that touch but do not overlap ***(Fig. 9)***. Come up at odd numbers and go down at even numbers.

Fig. 9

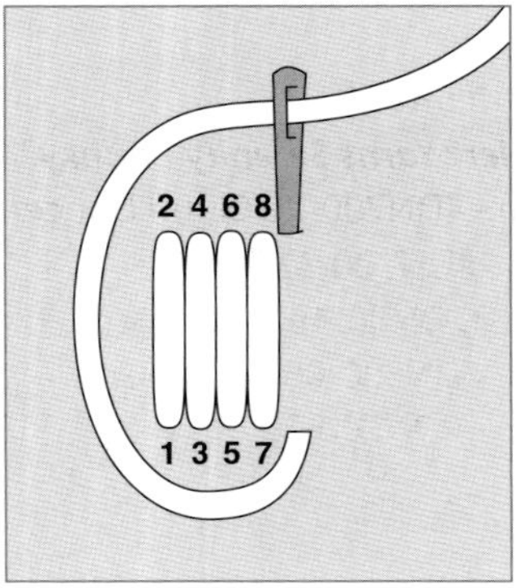

RUNNING STITCH

Running stitch is a series of straight stitches that weave in and out of the fabric. Come up at 1, go down at 2, come up at 3, and go down at 4 ***(Fig. 10)***. Continue in the same manner.

Fig. 10

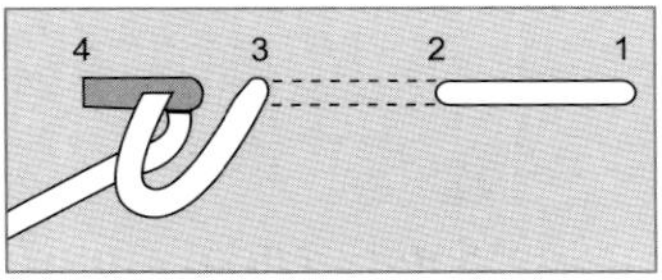

Yarn Information

The Snuggies in this book were made using a variety of yarns. Any brand of the specific weight of yarn may be used. It is best to refer to the yardage/ meters when determining how many balls or skeins to purchase. Remember, to achieve the same look, it is the weight of yarn that is important, not the brand of yarn.

For your convenience, listed below are the specific yarns used to create our photography models. Because yarn manufacturers make frequent changes to their product lines, you may sometimes find it necessary to use a substitute yarn or to search for the discontinued product at alternate suppliers (locally or online).

PRINCESS DRESS
Red Heart® Soft Essentials™
Purple - #7530 Sugar Plum
White - #7001 White

ICE CREAM CONE
Premier® Yarns Parfait™
Tan - #30-2 Toffee
Variegated - #31-11 Snow Cone

MERMAID TAIL
Red Heart® Sweet™
#0420 Seamist

PENCILS
Red Heart® Super Saver®
Yellow - #0324 Bright Yellow
Blue - #0886 Blue
Orange - #3251 Flame
Green - #0638 Paddy Green
Aran - #0313 Aran

PIZZA SLICE
Caron® One Pound™
Brown - #10611 Taupe
Yellow - #10546 Sunflower
Caron® Simply Soft™
Off White - #9702 Off White
Red - #9763 Harvest Red

WATERMELON SLICE
Lion Brand® Vanna's Choice®
Red - #133 Scarlet
Green - #172 Kelly Green
White - #100 White
Light Green - #171 Fern
Black - #153 Black

SUGAR SKULL
Premier® Yarns Serenity Chunky™
White - #DN700-20 Cloud Dancer
Black - #DN700-37 Raven
Blue - #7DN00-46 Blue Skies
Rose - #DN500-06 Berry Burst
Green - #DN700-39 Holly

Meet Lisa Gentry

A native of Germany who now resides in Louisiana, Lisa Gentry has been a crocheter since first grade. She came to the attention of the yarn industry after being awarded the title of Fastest Crocheter by the Guinness World Records in 2005. She was also later named America's fastest knitter by the Craft Yarn Council.

Since then, her knit and crochet designs have been prominently featured in top magazines and published in nearly 30 Leisure Arts books. Topics include crocodile stitch, chain knitting (a technique Lisa invented), ribbon crochet, women's sweaters, celebrity baby fashions, slouchy beanies for the family, urban hats knit with The Knook, cowls, neckwear, and more.

Look for other Leisure Arts books featuring Lisa's designs at www.leisurearts.com/meet-the-designers/lisa-gentry.html. For more about her designs, visit Ravelry.com and her company website, HookAndNeedleDesigns.com.

Production Team: Instructional/Technical Editor - Lois J. Long; Senior Graphic Artist - Lora Puls; Photo Stylist - Lori Wenger; and Photographer - Jason Masters.